DUDLEY SCHOOLS LIBRARY
AND INFORMATION SERVICE

KU-709-636

Schools Library and Information Services

S00000684741

CAN SCIENCE SOLVE?

THE MYSTERY OF
ATLANTIS

Holly Wallace

Heinemann
LIBRARY

www.heinemann.co.uk/library
Visit our website to find out more information about Heinemann Library books.

To order:
 Phone 44 (0) 1865 888112
Send a fax to 44 (0) 1865 314091
 Visit the Heinemann Bookshop at www.heinemann.co.uk/library to browse our
catalogue and order online.

First published in Great Britain by Heinemann Library, Halley Court, Jordan Hill, Oxford OX2 8EJ, part of Harcourt Education. Heinemann is a registered trademark of Harcourt Education Ltd.

© Harcourt Education Ltd 1999, 2006
The moral right of the proprietor has been asserted.

All rights reserved. No part of this publication may be reproduced, stored in a retrieval system, or transmitted in any form or by any means, electronic, mechanical, photocopying, recording, or otherwise, without either the prior written permission of the publishers or a licence permitting restricted copying in the United Kingdom issued by the Copyright Licensing Agency Ltd, 90 Tottenham Court Road, London W1T 4LP (www.cla.co.uk).

Editorial: Clare Lewis
Design: Victoria Bevan and Q2A
Production: Helen McCreath

Printed in China

10 digit ISBN 0 431 01885 5
13 digit ISBN 978 0 431 01885 0
10 09 08 07 06
10 9 8 7 6 5 4 3 2 1

British Library Cataloguing in Publication Data
Wallace, Holly
Can Science Solve: The Mystery of Atlantis – 2nd edition
001.9′4
A full catalogue record for this book is available from the British Library.

Acknowledgements
The publishers would like to thank the following for permission to reproduce photographs:
Ancient Art and Architecture Collection: p11, R Sheridan pp8, 18, 19, G Tortoli pp16, 20; Fortean Picture Library: pp7, 10, K Aarsleff p13, J and C Bord p22, W Donato pp25, 27, Llewellyn Publications p24; Ronald Grant Collection: p5; Oxford Scientific Films: R Packwood p14; Science Photo Library: p6, D Parker p12; Still Pictures: C Guarita p28.

Cover photograph of sand sculptures, Belgium, reproduced with permission of Empics/PA Photos/Reporters.

The publishers would like to thank Sarah Williams for her assistance in the preparation of this book.

Every effort has been made to contact copyright holders of any material reproduced in this book. Any omissions will be rectified in subsequent printings if notice is given to the publishers.

The paper used to print this book comes from sustainable resources.

DUDLEY PUBLIC LIBRARIES
L - - - - -
684741   SCH
J001.9

CONTENTS

UNSOLVED MYSTERIES   4

BEGINNINGS OF A MYSTERY   6

WHAT WAS ATLANTIS LIKE?   8

INTEREST RENEWED   10

OTHER THEORIES   12

ATLANTIS FOUND?   14

EARTH MOVEMENTS   16

LOOKING AT THE PAST   18

A VIOLENT VOLCANO   20

OTHER SUNKEN CITIES   22

STRANGE STORIES   24

A FALSE START   26

WHAT DO YOU THINK?   28

GLOSSARY   30

FIND OUT MORE   31

INDEX   32

UNSOLVED MYSTERIES

For hundreds of years, people have been interested in and puzzled by mysterious places, creatures and events. Is there really a monster living in Loch Ness? Are UFOs tricks of the light or actually vehicles from outer space? Who is responsible for mysterious crop circle patterns – clever hoaxers or alien beings? Did the lost land of Atlantis ever exist? Some of these mysteries have baffled scientists, who have spent years trying to find the answer. But just how far can science go? Are there some mysteries which science simply cannot solve? Read on, and make your own mind up...

In this book, you will learn about the lost land of Atlantis. Ever since the Greek writer Plato described Atlantis in the 4th century BC, there have been theories about the city and what happened to it. It also examines a range of theories about the city, dating from the 1880s right up to the 21st century. Read all the theories and then decide for yourself. Which one do you think is the most convincing?

What was Atlantis?

According to legend, Atlantis was an ancient island **civilization** in the Atlantic Ocean which existed about 12,000 years ago. Then, in the space of a night and a day, it sank without trace beneath the waves. It was a powerful kingdom, whose army had conquered large parts of Africa and Europe, before being defeated by the Ancient Greeks. Its people enjoyed a **privileged** lifestyle, surrounded by fine things and beautiful palaces. Until one fateful day, that is, when their golden world came crashing down around them.

But did Atlantis ever actually exist? We have no eyewitness reports to go by. No ruins have ever been found. Apart from one ancient account, later theories have often been based more in science fiction than in scientific fact. And if Atlantis did exist, two questions still remain – where was it located and how was it finally destroyed? Was it a natural disaster or an act of the gods? Is there anything science can do to solve one of the greatest mysteries of all?

Many books and films have been based on the story of Atlantis, including this one, entitled *The Lost Kingdom*. This is a scene inside the fabulous royal palace of the Atlantean king.

BEGINNINGS OF A MYSTERY

The first and only sources we have for the mystery of Atlantis are two ancient accounts, written by the Greek **philosopher** Plato in the 4th century BC. They are written as imaginary conversations which take place between the philosopher Socrates and three friends. The two accounts are called *Timaeus* and *Critias*, after their main characters. Plato began to work on a third account but it was never completed.

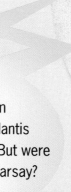

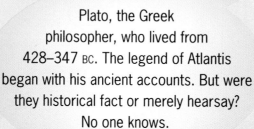

Plato, the Greek philosopher, who lived from 428–347 BC. The legend of Atlantis began with his ancient accounts. But were they historical fact or merely hearsay? No one knows.

Two accounts

In his version of events, Plato puts the story of Atlantis into the mouth of the poet and historian Critias. He says that he heard the story as a child from his grandfather, who had heard it from his own father. He, in turn, had heard it from his friend Solon (c640–558 BC), a famous Greek politician from Athens who had been told the story by an elderly Egyptian priest. By the priest's time, the story was already very old, recorded in the ancient temple records. It tells how, about 9,000 years before Solon's birth, or about 12,000 years ago, Atlantis was a rich, powerful island in the Atlantic Ocean whose armies conquered many of the lands around the Mediterranean until they were finally defeated by the Athenians. This is Plato's account of the Egyptian priest's words:

'There was an island situated in front of the **straits** which you call the Pillars of Hercules (now called the Straits of Gibraltar) and which was larger than Libya and Asia Minor (modern Turkey) put together... . Now on this island of Atlantis there was a great and wonderful **empire** which ruled over the whole island and several others, and over parts of the **continent**, and controlled, within the straits, Libya as far as Egypt and Europe as far as Tyrrhenia (Italy). This vast power attempted to **subdue** both my country (Egypt) and yours (Greece) and the whole region within the strait. Then, Solon, your country defeated the invaders and saved us all from slavery. But afterwards, there occurred violent earthquakes and floods, and in a single day and night, the island of Atlantis was swallowed up by the sea and disappeared...'

A map of Atlantis from the 1644 book, *Mundus Subterraneus* [The Underground World], by Dutch writer Athanasius Kircher. He based his guess at Atlantis' location on Plato's accounts.

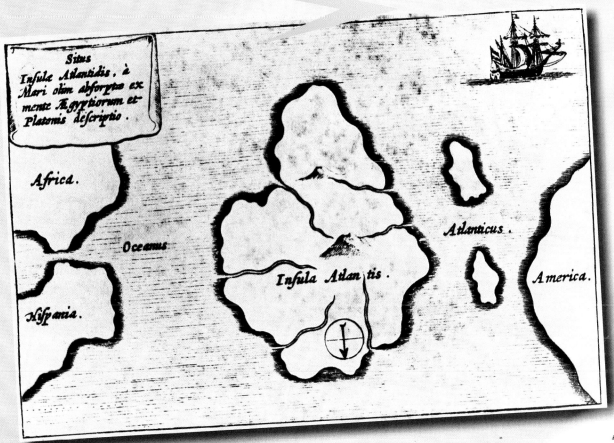

Situs Insulæ Atlantidis, à Mari olim absorptæ ex mente Ægyptiorum et Platonis descriptio.

Africa.

Oceanus.

Hispania.

Insula Atlantis.

Atlanticus.

America.

INTEREST RENEWED

Modern interest in Atlantis began in the 19th century with the publication, in 1882, of an extraordinary book called *Atlantis, the Antediluvian World*. Written by an American politician, Ignatius Donnelly, the book quickly became a best-seller all over the world. The cult of Atlantis was born.

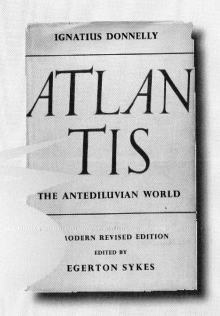

IGNATIUS DONNELLY

ATLAN TIS

THE ANTEDILUVIAN WORLD

MODERN REVISED EDITION
EDITED BY
EGERTON SYKES

The cover of Donnelly's best-selling book, *Atlantis, the Antediluvian World*. It sparked off a huge amount of interest in the mystery of Atlantis.

Donnelly's theory

Donnelly firmly believed that Atlantis had existed and that it had perished exactly as Plato described. He placed the island in the Azores in the mid-Atlantic (see page 16) and made the following claims to back up his theory:

- A large island, Atlantis, once existed in the Atlantic Ocean. It was all that remained of an Atlantic **continent**.

- Plato's description was historical fact.

- **Civilization** itself began in Atlantis.

- Atlantis was a mighty power which conquered many other countries.

- It was the true antediluvian world.

- The oldest colony founded by the Atlanteans was in Egypt.

- The Atlanteans were the first people to use iron and bronze.

- The Atlanteans invented the first alphabet.

- Atlantis was destroyed by a natural disaster, such as an earthquake or volcanic eruption.

- A few people escaped on rafts and ships.

A lack of evidence

Donnelly based his theories on his reading of Plato's account of Atlantis and in his own study of a variety of sciences, including **zoology** and **geology**. In the 19th century, these 'new sciences' were beginning to be studied and taken seriously for the first time. His claims captured the imagination of a great many people but serious scientists dismissed them as nonsense. After all, there was no hard evidence whatsoever to back them up.

Sun worship

From his study of ancient religions, Donnelly concluded that the people of Atlantis worshipped the Sun and that their religion spread to Ancient Egypt and Peru. Since then, **archaeologists** have discovered many Egyptian paintings showing worship of the Sun god, Ra, and mysterious carvings of the Sun in the Nazca desert in Peru. Could Donnelly's claims be true?

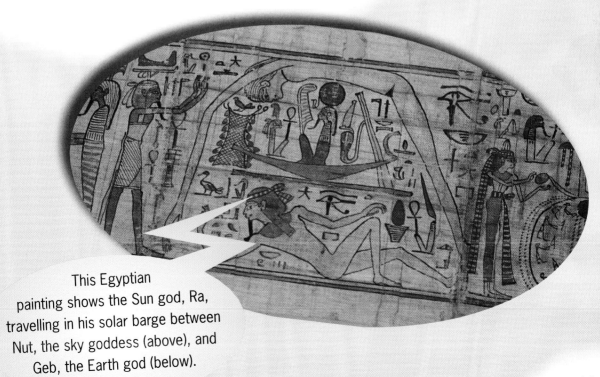

This Egyptian painting shows the Sun god, Ra, travelling in his solar barge between Nut, the sky goddess (above), and Geb, the Earth god (below).

OTHER THEORIES

Although many people dismissed Donnelly's book as pure speculation, it sparked off a massive amount of interest in Atlantis. Thousands of books, articles and short stories followed, and the name of Atlantis was used on everything from ships to a region of the planet Mars. There were hundreds of other theories too, some based, if loosely, in science; others completely made up. Here are just some of them...

This huge crater in Arizona, USA, was formed when a giant meteorite hit the Earth some 50,000 years ago. Could an even larger meteorite have caused Atlantis to sink?

Bombardment from space

Several theories suggest that Atlantis was destroyed by an enormous **meteorite** hitting the Earth. In 1976, German scientist and engineer, Otto Muck, published his book *The Secret of Atlantis*. In it he points to two huge depressions, seven kilometres deep, on the sea floor in the western Atlantic, as likely **impact craters**. Scientifically, this could have been possible – in 1920, a meteorite weighing 59 tonnes struck Namibia in Africa, the largest meteorite yet known. But Muck calculates that the Atlantic meteorite must have been 10 kilometres wide and claims that it also split the Atlantic Ocean open along the line of the Mid-Atlantic Ridge, a long chain of underwater mountains running down the middle of the Atlantic Ocean. Science has since proved this to be untrue (see pages 16–17).

Evidence from eels

In his book Muck also suggested that the sinking of Atlantis could explain the mysterious **migrations** of eels across the Atlantic. Each year, European eels leave their river homes and swim across the Atlantic to the Sargasso Sea to breed. Then the tiny **elvers** begin an incredible 6,000-kilometre, three-year-long journey home, carried on the warm waters of the Gulf Stream current. Muck wondered why the eels should risk such a long and dangerous journey? He suggested that the Gulf Stream once circled Atlantis and carried the eels to fresh water by a much shorter, more direct route. When Atlantis sank, it broke the flow of the Gulf Stream and made the eels' journey much longer.

Pyramid parallels

Some people, including Lewis Spence, a writer from Scotland, tried to link Atlantis to the **civilizations** of Central and South America. Between the 1920s and the 1940s, he wrote several books pointing to similarities between, for example, the pyramids built by the Mayas in Mexico and those built by the Ancient Egyptians, whose country was supposedly ruled by Atlantis. But many historians do not believe that the two are linked.

A Mayan pyramid in Mexico. Because it was similar in shape to the pyramids of Ancient Egypt, supposedly a colony of Atlantis, Spence suggested that its building may have been influenced by Atlantean culture.

13

ATLANTIS FOUND?

So, if Atlantis did exist, where was it located? According to Plato, 'it was an island situated in front of the **straits** which are called the Pillars of Hercules'. This places it to the west of the Straits of Gibraltar (called the Pillars of Hercules by the Greeks) in the Atlantic Ocean. But not everyone agrees. Some of the other locations suggested for Atlantis include America, Scandinavia, the Canary Islands and even Greenland. You can read more about possible locations on the following pages.

Spanish lands

In 2004, Dr Rainer Kuehne suggested that the lost 'island' of Atlantis was once a large region off the southwest coast of Spain. This sunken area was swamped by a **tsunami**, around 12,000 years ago. This is roughly the same time as the earthquake and floods that Plato described swallowing up Atlantis. The sunken Spanish lands lie close to the Straits of Gibraltar - exactly where Plato said Atlantis could be found. However, these lands were originally part of Spain, while Plato wrote about an island.

The summit of the Rock of Gibraltar. In ancient times, this rock and Mount Hacho, in modern Morocco, were known as the Pillars of Hercules, marking the division between the Mediterranean Sea and the Atlantic Ocean.

Satellite evidence?

In 2005, pictures were taken by a satellite camera, showing the ocean bed off the southwest coast of Spain. These pictures may support Dr Kuehne's theory that Atlantis was once part of Spain. The satellite pictures appear to show some large, rectangular buildings and some tall walls. Could these be the ruins of the great city described by Plato?

Northern Europe

In his 1976 book, *Atlantis of the North*, German scholar, Dr Jürgen Spanuth tried to prove that Atlantis was located off the north-west coast of Germany where there was a group of sunken islands. He also claimed that the people of Atlantis were, in fact, the early ancestors of the Vikings. But no evidence has yet been found to support his claim.

Antarctic Atlantis

American author, Alan F Alford suggested in his 1996 book *Gods of the New Millennium*, that Atlantis may have been situated in Antarctica. He says that, at the time given by Plato for Atlantis's existence, which was about 12,000 years ago, Antarctica was ice free. When the region did freeze over, which was about 6,000 years ago according to Alford, its people (the Atlanteans) spread far and wide throughout the world, including Egypt where they built the pyramids. It is true that Antarctica was not always a frozen **continent**. It once had a much warmer climate than today. But from the **geological** study of ancient rock and ice samples, scientists know that Antarctica was largely covered in ice two to three million years ago, so Alford's theory could not be correct.

LOOKING AT THE PAST

One of the most believable theories about the location of Atlantis places it in the Mediterranean Sea, on the Greek island of Crete. It was here, about 4,000 years ago, that a mighty civilization grew up, which showed many similarities with Plato's Atlantis. Could they be one and the same? Some scientists think they might be.

Part of the ruined Minoan palace of Knossos. Some scientists believe that the Atlanteans and Minoans may have been one and the same people.

Rediscovering the Minoans

Our knowledge of the Minoans, the people who lived on Crete some 4,000 years ago, comes from archaeological evidence found on Crete. In 1900, British **archaeologist**, Sir Arthur Evans, began excavating the magnificent royal palace at Knossos. He uncovered a civilization far more advanced and sophisticated than anything yet found in Europe. Evans called it Minoan after a **legendary** ruler, King Minos.

Similarities ...

From Evans' discoveries, other scholars drew similarities between Minoan and Atlantean culture. The Minoans built their towns around magnificent royal palaces. The largest and grandest was at Knossos. Did Plato hear about this and base his description of the royal palace in Atlantis on it? Or had the story reached the Ancient Egyptians, who had passed it to Solon as Plato claimed (see pages 6–9)?

A **fresco** from Knossos showing the ancient sport of bull-leaping. Both the Atlanteans and Minoans were said to have worshipped bulls as sacred animals.

Evans also found many paintings and sculptures of bulls which were sacred animals for the Minoans. Plato described a similar **cult** of bull-worship on Atlantis.

Finally, both the Minoans and Atlanteans met a mysterious and violent end. In about 1500 BC, Minoan civilization was destroyed by a series of natural disasters, including earthquakes and tidal waves. Similar to the 'violent earthquakes and floods' which Plato says destroyed Atlantis...

... and differences

So could Crete be Atlantis? Despite the similarities, there are problems with the theory. Firstly, Crete was not a round island, as Plato described Atlantis to be, and it did not sink beneath the sea and vanish without trace. Secondly, it is not located in the Atlantic. However, Minoan script, called Linear A, found on clay tablets and discs from Crete, is not yet fully understood by archaeologists. Who knows what secrets it might hold...

A VIOLENT VOLCANO

Many experts have linked the collapse of Minoan civilization to the violent eruption of Thera, a volcanic island about 110 kilometres to the north of Crete. Or could Thera itself have been Atlantis?

Excavations at Akrotiri on Santorini (Thera) have uncovered a great city in Minoan style. Could these be the long-lost ruins of Atlantis?

Thera erupts

The traditional date given for the eruption of Thera is 1450 BC, about the same time as the Minoan collapse. So violent was the explosion that most of Thera was blown away, leaving only a small, crescent-shaped island which is now also called Santorini. This may have caused tidal waves, flooding and earth tremors on Crete. Recent **archaeological** evidence suggests, however, that Thera may have erupted some 200 years earlier and may not have been responsible for the destruction of Minoan Crete. Even if these two dates matched, they still placed the destruction of Atlantis just 900 years before Solon, not 9000 as Plato claimed.

Thera as Atlantis

So, could Thera have been the **catastrophe** which destroyed Atlantis?
Greek **archaeologist** Professor Spyridon Marinatos certainly thought
so. He also believed that Thera was linked to Crete, possibly as a result
of the spread of Minoan culture throughout the Mediterranean. In 1967,
he began excavating at Akrotiri, in the south west of Santorini (Thera).
Buried under layers of volcanic ash, Marinatos found the remains of a
great city, with streets of Minoan-style houses and **frescos** showing a
highly advanced civilization. As for the problem of dates, he suggested
a scribe (writer) had simply written the wrong dates down, multiplying
everything by 10.

Another possibility is that Thera itself was Atlantis. After all, scientists
know that, during the eruption which destroyed the island, the central
part of the island sank into the sea.

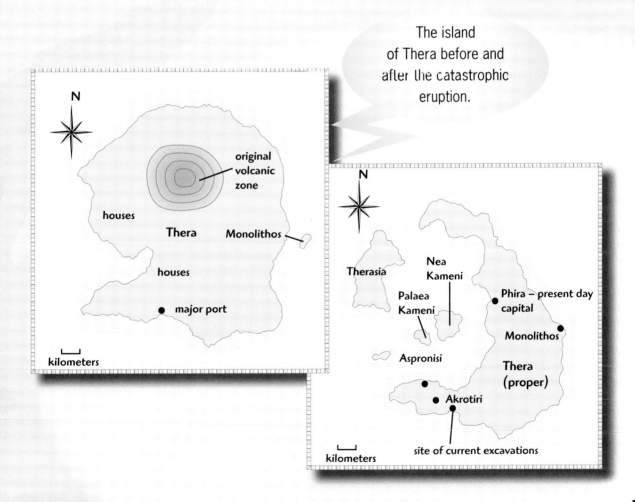

The island
of Thera before and
after the catastrophic
eruption.

STRANGE STORIES

As you have seen, there are many different theories about Atlantis. Some have been very carefully thought out, taking science and history into account to try to solve the mystery. Often, unfortunately, the science used has since been proved wrong. Other theories are much, much stranger, without any basis in science at all. Many have been put forward by people called **occultists** whose interest lies in the world of the supernatural.

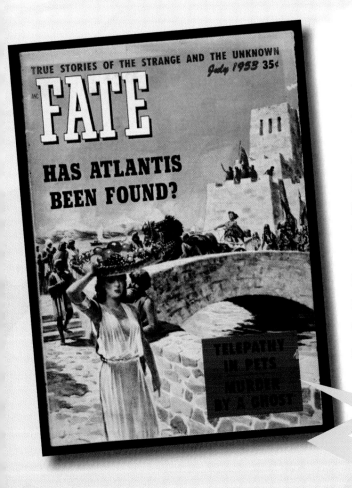

TRUE STORIES OF THE STRANGE AND THE UNKNOWN
July 1953 35¢

FATE

HAS ATLANTIS BEEN FOUND?

TELEPATHY IN PETS
MURDER BY A GHOST

Atlantis rising

Atlantology is the name given to the study, scientific or otherwise, of Atlantis. Many Atlantologists believe that, one day, Atlantis will rise again. This may not mean that the island will physically rise from the sea but that there will be a return of the qualities and virtues of goodness, courage and wisdom which made Atlantis great. The only question is ... when?

Despite many theories having been disproved, the possibility of finding Atlantis still excites both **archaeologists** and those interested in the supernatural.

The fourth race

In 1877, Russian occultist, Helena Blavatsky published a huge book, called *Isis Unveiled*. It contained just one page on Atlantis. In it, Madame Blavatsky claimed that the people of Atlantis were the fourth 'race' on Earth, a super-human people who lived long before the present human beings, and who had amazing **psychic** powers. But they were corrupted by a great dragon king, Thevetat, and turned into wicked magicians. They began a war which ended with Atlantis being submerged.

In her next book, *The Secret Doctrine*, published after she died, Madame Blavatsky had more to say. The book is a commentary on an ancient text said to have been actually written in Atlantis. Among her many claims, she tells how the survivors of Atlantis settled in Egypt and built the pyramids about 100,000 years ago. But modern science shows that the earliest were actually built in about 2600 BC.

A huge stone statue of a Toltec warrior.

Toltec ancestors

In the 1890s, another occultist, W Scott-Elliott claimed to be able to read the so-called 'Akasic Records'. These were a secret history of ancient wisdom, said to exist on the astral plane, in another dimension beyond normal life. From his reading, he claimed that Atlantis had existed an incredible one million years ago. There were seven races of Atlanteans, one of which was the Toltecs. In conventional history, the Toltecs were a nomadic people of Mexico. They built their capital at Tula, north of Mexico City, in about AD 900.

A FALSE START

In the 1920s, an American clairvoyant, Edgar Cayce, claimed that he had spent one of his past lives in Atlantis. According to him, Atlantis reached from the Sargasso Sea to the Azores and was about the size of Europe. Its land and civilization had been destroyed twice, in the course of which the mainland had been split into islands. The last to sink was near the Bahamas. In 1940, Cayce predicted that this part of Atlantis would rise again, some time around 1968. But was he right?

Fakes and frauds

In the 1870s, German archaeologist, Heinrich Schliemann, discovered the ruins of the ancient city of Troy in Turkey, the site of the **legendary** Trojan War. Forty years later, his grandson, Paul, claimed that Troy and Atlantis had been allies. He said that his grandfather had found a bowl at Troy, inscribed with the words 'From King Cronos of Atlantis'. Archaeologists later proved that the bowl was a fake.

The Bimini Road

Early in 1968, an **archaeologist**, Dr J Manson Valentine, found a J-shaped pathway of rectangular stone slabs about 700 metres long and lying several metres underwater off the coast of North Bimini, in the Bahamas. It became known as the Bimini Road. There was great excitement. Had Atlantis been found, as Cayce had predicted? One Atlantis-hunter had no doubt. He claimed that the stones were part of an ancient Atlantean temple. One of them might even be the head of a stone statue.

Scientists disagreed. Some said that the pavement had been formed naturally. Others accepted that it could be man-made but was likely to be the remains of a sea wall which had sunk beneath the water. In 1981, in the course of an **oceanographic** survey of the area, the US Geological Survey solved at least part of the mystery by proving that the 'Road' had indeed been laid down by natural means between 2500 and 3500 years ago, long after Atlantis.

A glimpse of the Bimini Road. You can just pick out the J-shaped pathway of stones beneath the water.

GLOSSARY

antediluvian the time before the flood. There are many myths about a great flood sent by the gods to punish people for becoming wicked. Before this, they lived for centuries in peace and happiness in paradise.

archaeologist scientist who studies the past by looking at ancient ruins and remains

artefact ancient object, such as a pot, a piece of jewellery or a weapon, which helps to tell archaeologists about the past

catastrophe a sudden, widespread disaster

civilization a people and the society they live in

clairvoyant a person who claims to have the power to look into the future

continent a large mass of land

cult a religious group

echo sounder an instrument used to measure the depth of the water and to map the features of the sea bed. It gives out pulses of sound which hit parts of the sea-floor and send back echoes. The pattern of the echoes is traced on to a screen to create a picture of the sea-floor.

elver a young eel

empire a large group of countries ruled by one, strong power

fresco a painting drawn on wet plaster

geology the scientific study of the rocks of the Earth's crust

impact crater a deep hollow in the ground left when a meteorite hits the Earth

legendary based on a legend, which may or may not be true

meteorite a lump of space rock which originally comes from comets and which sometimes crashes into the Earth

migration a long journey made by some fish, birds and mammals between their feeding and breeding grounds

occultist a person who is interested in the supernatural

oceanography the study of the oceans. It is a mixture of different sciences – biology, geology, chemistry, physics and meteorology.

philosopher a person who studies the meaning behind life and the Universe. In Ancient Greek times, a philosopher was someone who studied all aspects of the world around them.

pinnacle a decorative turret on a building's roof

privileged lucky or honoured

psychic a person who claims to be able to read people's minds and to see into the future

radar an instrument used to detect the direction, range and presence of objects which show up on a screen

strait a narrow channel connecting two large areas of water

subdue to put down

tsunami large wave caused by an earthquake under the sea or an underwater volcanic eruption

zoology the scientific study

Find out more

You can find out more about the Atlantis in books and on the Internet. Use a search engine such as www.yahooligans.com to search for information. A search for the words "Atlantis" will bring back lots of results, but it may be difficult to find the information you want. Try refining your search to look for some of the people and ideas mentioned in this book, such as "Seven Sisters" or "Helena Blavatsky".

More Books to Read

Eyewitness Readers: Atlantis: The Lost City, Andrew Donkin (Dorling Kindersley, 2000)

Out There? Mysteries of the Deep, John Townsend (Raintree, 2004)

Websites

http://theshadowlands.net/atlantis/

http://www.crystalinks.com/atlantis.html

INDEX

Alford, Alan F   15
Antarctica   15
Apollonia   22
archaeology   4, 11, 18, 19, 20, 21, 23, 26
Athens   6, 28
Atlantis
    civilization   4, 8, 9, 10, 18, 19
    destruction of   7, 9, 10, 26
    films about   5
    location of   7, 10, 13, 14, 15, 26
Azores   10, 16, 17

Bahamas   26
Bimini Road   26, 27, 29
Blavatsky, Madame Helena   25
Brazil   14, 29
bull worship   19

Cayce, Edgar   26
Crete   18, 19, 20, 28, 29

diving   23
Donnelly, Ignatius   10, 11, 12, 16, 17

Earth's crust   16, 17
eels   13
Egypt   6, 7, 10, 11, 13, 29
Evans, Sir Arthur   18
Fawcett, Percy   14

geology   11, 15, 16, 17
Greece   4, 6, 7, 28

Libya   7, 28
Lyonesse   22

Marinatos, Professor Spyridon   21
meteorite   12
Mexico   13, 25
Mid-Atlantic Ridge   12, 16
Muck, Otto   12, 13

occultists   24, 25
oceanography   17

Peru   11, 29
Pillars of Hercules   7, 14
Plato   4, 6, 8, 9, 10, 11, 14, 18, 20, 28, 29
Port Royal   23
Poseidon   8, 9
pyramids   13

Socrates   6
Solon   6, 7, 9, 18, 20, 28
Spanuth, Dr Jürgen   15
Spence, Lewis   13
Sun worship   11

Thera   20, 21, 29
Toltecs   25
Troy   26

Wegener, Alfred   17

Zeus   9
zoology   11